BARNS

BARNS

Their History, Preservation, and Restoration

TEXT AND PHOTOGRAPHS BY
CHARLES KLAMKIN

BONANZA BOOKS

New York

Library of Congress Cataloging in Publication Data

Klamkin, Charles.
Barns, their history, preservation, and restoration.
Includes index.
1. Barns. I. Title.
NA8230.K55 1979   728′.9   70-16099
ISBN 0-517-29723-X

For Marian

Acknowledgments

I would like to express my gratitude to Dan Calabrese, whose enthusiasm for my barn photographs prompted the idea of putting them together in a book. Also, I would like to thank William Watkins, Director, Mattatuck Museum, Waterbury, Connecticut, and John A. Coe, of Middlebury, Connecticut, for allowing me to photograph early tools from their collections. I especially appreciate the gracious cooperation of Mr. and Mrs. Roger Barnes, Michael Wager, and Peter Fink, who allowed me to photograph the barns that they have converted into magnificent homes. I would also like to thank Eric Sloane, whose research and many books dealing with the tools, building materials, architecture, and customs of this country's early history provide a source of inspiration for all workers in this field.

C. K.

Contents

BARNS

CHAPTER 1

Save the Barns

WHY should anyone be concerned about the decay, destruction, and demise of old New England barns? The purposes for which they were originally built are now obsolete in today's economy and technology. The farming still being carried on in the area is only marginally profitable and depends to a great extent upon specialization. We have dairy farmers, potato and tobacco growers, some orchards, and a few farms that still raise vegetables in commerical quantities.

The barns needed for this kind of farming are very different from the ones put up by the original settlers of the land and convey more of an industrial than an agricultural aspect. The barns that are disappearing were built by men who cleared the rocks and trees from their land and then built their barns with the same native materials. Their barns were products of their own needs, industry, and imagination. Although there may appear to be a certain degree of sameness among old, unpainted, weathered barns, each one has its own special character.

Barns in New England vary in the way they are situated on the land and oriented to the weather, in the shading of the wood from gray to brown, and in the small details of design. One barn may have a jog built onto it to house a few additional head of livestock or a carriage shed which may have been added by a later generation. Another will display an unusual cupola or elaborate window design. A few will give evidence of less meticulous construction or preservation in their swaybacked roofs or wind-bent frames.

It is just this individuality and mark of handcraftsmanship that we miss in the commercial and residential architecture of today. The standards we apply to the best contemporary architecture are all present in the design of the early New England barns. Nowhere in American architecture is there a better example of function governing the form of a building. Without elaborate plans and using unsophisticated tools and materials, the builders were interested only in enclosing a suitable place for their livestock with as sound and economical a structure as possible. They took the stone and timber from the fields they were clearing and incorporated them into their barns. Each farmer built his barn according to the number and type of animals he owned and located his barn in relation to the contours of the land.

This individuality in terms of a barn's size, design, and construction is the main reason they charm us now. Yet despite their differences, each barn had a symmetry and relationship in its proportions that carried over into the architecture of the best homes of the period. An example of this can be found in the so-called saltbox houses which are a derivation of early barn design.

The principal aesthetic appeal of an old barn lies in the feeling of essential rightness. Its site on the land, its orientation to the weather, the structural proportions, and the use of materials all contribute to this sense of harmony. We know instinctively that all the elements in its construction blended to create a structure truly appropriate to its surroundings and to the purpose for which it was built.

The barns of the eighteenth and early nineteenth centuries were not built as showplaces or architectural monuments. They were erected out of necessity, often before the owners' dwellings were fully completed. Regardless of a man's trade or profession in Colonial times, everyone farmed the land he lived on. Farm animals, particularly oxen and horses, were essential in performing the heavy work, and a few cows, fowl, and swine were kept for food. The New England climate dictated that these animals had to have proper shelter in the winter months, and the barn performed that function as well as providing storage for their fodder. Since these farmers depended to such a great extent upon the condition of their livestock, the animals' well-being often superseded the immediate comfort considerations of the family.

It is now over one hundred years since the basic economy of New England began its change from an agricultural to an industrial one. As the towns and cities grew, more and more farmland was appropriated for housing and factories. The bulk of the population shifted from the farms to urban tenements and suburban housing developments. The growth of suburban towns converted thousands of farms into building lots, and now shopping centers and highways occupy the remainder of this formerly rural real estate. The few remaining farms are unable to provide a reasonable livelihood for their owners. Most of these will be gone in the next generation.

Although the old New England barns are rapidly disappearing, there seems to be an almost instinctive impulse among many people to preserve some of their virtues. Siding removed from these barns has become an extremely popular building material. Apparently, the decorative effect of the aged wood with its mellowness and patina cannot be duplicated in plywood paneling. The demand for these weathered boards for finishing basement playrooms and dens has caused its price to skyrocket and has accelerated the dismantling of the few old barns still standing.

There is also an appreciation of the merit of converting old barns into homes. It is a way of securing a dwelling with a degree of space, soundness, and charm that is impossible with today's building methods and materials. The prices of old barns suitable for conversion have risen greatly in the past several years. It is often cheaper, however, to remodel such a structure than to construct a new house of equal size. With time, patience, and affection, these restorations can produce a much more satisfying home.

3

Barns   Before too many more New England barns are torn down, stripped for siding, or allowed to crumble away, some record should be made of what we are losing and why they will be missed. Through the photographs and text of this book I hope to convey a sense of the strength, simplicity, and adaptability of these structures as well as the character of their builders.

Signs like this are found on barns all over New England as farms are abandoned and the buildings stripped or left to decay.

6 Some barns can disappear in a season or two. Connecticut barn overlooking cornfield in autumn.

Low winter sun in December seeps through the missing boards.

By spring most of the siding has disappeared and the attached shed has collapsed. Only the frame and roof are still standing.

7

Once graceful barn in Tyringham, Massachusetts, fights to remain upright.

8

Six months later the Tyringham barn has lost the battle, and this pile of rubble is all that is left.

Now empty but essentially intact and fully equipped dairy barn waits for the wreckers.

Bulldozer moves toward the cow stanchions in what remains of dairy barn in previous photograph.

This building started life in the first half of the nineteenth century as a tin-smith's factory in Hotchkissville, Connecticut. A barn would not have been built with so many windows. It is still a rural ornament as a place to store hay from the fields surrounding it.

Inside, the light falling on the stacked hay bales creates a quiet feeling far removed from present-day tension.

This abandoned barn struggles against the winter wind to remain standing. It survived the elements but succumbed to building lots.

The siding has already been stripped from this tobacco barn in Suffield, Connecticut. In the background can be seen part of the housing development that has hastened the demise of these barns.

Swaybacked barns are not hard to find, as roofs are not renewed, and ridge poles decay.

Even after a barn has outlived its usefulness, it still has more aesthetic value than a billboard.

Siding randomly taken from this old Vermont dairy barn leaves Mondrian-like patterns.

Skeleton of this Vermont barn overlooks fifty-mile view of the Green Mountains.
At left can be seen remains of barn's grain room.

Only the graceful curves in the loft window soften the severe lines of this Massachusetts barn.

Aging barn looks like mattress losing its stuffing.

Older buildings on Connecticut dairy farm crumble while more recent well-built silo will stand for years or until it, too, is torn down.

For Sale sign is up on this property in Bridgewater, Connecticut. Barn is over 150 years old and was built on foundation of unusually large uncemented stones.

The burden of too many seasons of winter snow has collapsed the roof of this long-unused wagon shed.

24

Large turn-of-the-century barn is carefully dismantled to salvage as much of the lumber as possible.

Man at work stripping siding from barn being razed to make way for a housing development. "Board and batten" construction with a narrow strip nailed over the joints in the siding slows the wrecking process.

26

CHAPTER 2

How the Old Barns Were Built

OLD barns are landmarks today. Many have managed to survive because they were so well constructed. The choice of location where the barn was to be placed was the first consideration. Ideally, the ground should have had some elevation above the surrounding terrain to facilitate drainage and to make excavation easier in case a basement was included.

If livestock were to be kept in the barn, a supply of fresh water had to be available from a nearby pond or brook. The direction of the prevailing winds in the colder months had to be borne in mind so that the front of the barn could be oriented away from the weather. This reduced the possibility of snow piling up against the entrance and preventing access to the barn.

The earliest barns built in New England in the seventeenth century were adaptations of European types and were designed principally for the storage of grain. The building was low and expanded horizontally as more space was required for the shelter of animals. Roofs were steeply pitched to accommodate the thatching that was universally used for covering.

This type of construction was soon abandoned as the American farmer began to design barns that were better suited to the more rigorous climate of New England. Thatch gave way to shingles for roofs, and barn heights were raised to enclose a greater space within a more compact, less spread-out structure.

27

The time in the eighteenth century when barns with an elevated profile began to appear was also the period when farm livestock began to be kept in increasing numbers. The original settlers were concerned mainly with raising crops of corn and grains, and the labor was almost entirely manual. They did not keep domestic animals; meat was plentiful simply by hunting and trapping.

As better farming practices developed, animals, principally oxen, became widely used for pulling plows and hauling heavy loads. Shelter for these animals was incorporated within the taller structure by providing space for them at the bottom level to facilitate moving them in and out and for the simpler cleaning of their quarters. The floor above the animals was reserved for storing grain and fodder on both sides of a central open space. This unobstructed area in the middle was used for threshing grain to separate the kernels from the chaff. In the spaces on each side of the threshing floor were bays or mows to store the sheaves of grain before it was threshed or to hold the straw after the kernels were removed. Part of the loft was used to keep hay for the animals. When the hay was to be fed to the livestock, it was a simple matter to pitch it into an opening or stairwell and let it fall to the barn floor below, where it could be distributed.

These two-story barns were usually built into the side of a hill so that both floors were accessible from ground levels. This permitted wagons to be driven directly into the upper, or threshing, floor, to facilitate loading and unloading. It also saved the builders the trouble and expense of constructing heavy ramps.

Clearing the site for a new barn was one of the more arduous tasks entailed in its construction. This meant felling trees, pulling stumps, and removing tons of stone. If the barn was to be built into a hillside, enough excavation had to be done to provide for the front elevation. With nothing but pickaxes, shovels, and crowbars earth and rock were removed and the foundation built up from the always present stone previously removed from the site. The stones in the foundation were so carefully fitted that most often no mortar was used. That is probably why one can still find remains of these foundations long after the barns they supported have disappeared. Cemented foundations will in time crumble as the mortar, which is not as durable as stone, deteriorates.

Extending across the center of the foundation and spanning its longest dimension, a girder was placed in a niche left in the stonework to receive it. This left the top surface of the girder flush with the top of the foundation. The girder, supported by a few guide posts of stone or timber along its length, was the main bearing member supporting the floor and a great deal of superstructure. Since great strength was required for this member, oak beams up to twelve inches square were chosen.

Around the top of the foundation, wooden beams called the sill were placed. Notches or recesses were cut into the sill to position the horizontal floor beams which extended across the shorter dimension of the foundation and were supported in the middle by the main girder. The sills were also notched out or mortised at the corners and in several places along their length to receive the vertical beam, which were erected after the floorboards had been laid across the floor beams.

All of these heavy timbers from six to eight to twelve inches square and ranging upward to thirty feet in length were fashioned at the site without recourse to a sawmill. Yet they are straight and square and were made by skilled craftsmen using only two different types of axes. First, a series of horizontal cuts was made on four sides along the length of the log with a narrow-bladed ax with a thick bit. Then the woodsman would work down the log with his broadax. This wide-bladed, thin-edged tool chopped away the bark and wood between the transverse cuts, leaving a squared-off beam.

With the sills and floor beams laid it was then time to erect the barn frame. Instead of installing the upright posts one at a time into the sills and then tying them together with bracing, this heavy framing was done in sections on the ground. These frame sections, called bents, are analogous to ribs in an animal. The bent was a complete unit of framework, fully braced and extended from the sill to the point where the roof was attached. The bent was as wide as the width of the barn and from eight to sixteen feet high.

Constructing the bents called for the only real skill and precision in the barn-building process. Distances had to be accurately measured and the mortises carefully made to receive adjoining members. All of the joining of these thick supporting timbers was done by fitting one member into another with chiseled-out mortises and tenons. Pieces were fastened to each other by driving them together with a heavy wooden mallet weighing up to forty pounds. This mallet was called a beetle.

This joining technique is much like the dovetailing we look for in the corners of drawers in a well-made piece of furniture. Where the beams were joined, they were locked by driving an oak peg into a hole bored through both timbers. This method was much stronger and definitely less costly than using iron spikes or nails. Most of the old barns still standing were built in this fashion.

After the required number of bents were made, from a minimum of four to as many as the length of the barn required, it was then necessary to raise and position them vertically in the mortises provided in the sill. This would be an early example of prefabricated building methods.

Raising these bents made up of several heavy eight-by-eight-inch timbers required more manpower than was ordinarily available on the job. This called for bringing in friends and neighbors from miles around to help lift the bents into place. Men would come with their wives and children, bringing their own tools and tackle. The most useful tool was a long stout pole fifteen to twenty feet long with a sharp iron spike protruding from one end. This was called a pike and was used to raise and hold the bents upright until they could be firmly anchored and braced. Ropes and pulleys were employed in lifting the bents off the ground. With the manpower donated as a free communal effort it was the obligation of the owner of the new barn to provide plenty of food and drink for all. Although much hard work was involved, these barn-raisings were looked forward to as a party and a break in the onerous routine of the early New England farm families.

In a book on barn construction entitled *Barn Plans and Outbuildings*, first published in 1881, the author, Dr. Byron D. Halsted, suggests reasons why the old methods gave way to the new: "With the scarcity of heavy timber and consequent cost it is time farmers who are to erect barns should give some study to the newer methods of framing, where no timber is thicker than two inches and from six to eight inches wide. It is about half as costly, and a first class carpenter is not required to erect it."

Where greater strength was required, builders were advised to spike together two or three of these two-by-eight-inch boards, making the equivalent of a four- or six-by-eight-inch beam. We can assume, then, that by the latter part of the nineteenth century the tall, thick timber required for the traditional type of frame had been pretty well cut over. Also, the craftsmen who could trim, square, and notch such beams and then join them soundly without a nail were becoming scarcer.

Once the frame, or bents, was up, the neighbors departed, and the work of fastening the siding and making a roof was left to the farmer and his sons or hired men. The siding was usually made of pine, which could easily be sawed into boards at a local sawmill. Early sawmills operated with a straight vertical saw or a gang of them driven by water power. These vertical saws with their up and down motion left a characteristic striation on the face of the boards cut in that manner. Very few such boards can be found today, since the sawmills converted to the circular saw around 1820 after it was introduced by the Shakers.

Other indications of the approximate age of an old barn can be determined by an examination of the construction of the roof and its covering. Early roof rafters were joined at the peak in the same way as the bents. That is, where they met at the peak, they were fitted together with a mortise and tenon, and a wooden pin was driven through the two rafters. Later, the rafters were fastened to a ridge pole or board which ran the length of the roof. This was concurrent with the greater availability of nails, which began to be produced by machine around 1790.

Earliest roofs were covered with shingles provided by bark stripped from trees, preferably cedar. These were laid in an overlapping pattern with one shingle with the bark side down and the next with the bark side up, very much in the manner of roof tiles in Spanish architecture. Better shingles, easier to apply, were later made by splitting a two- or three-foot section of pine, oak, or cedar logs into wide, thin sections. The splitting was accomplished quite simply by placing a dull metal blade called a froe at the top of the log and striking it with a mallet. Some of these hand-riven shingles still provide good protection from the weather.

Testimony to the quality of wood used and the care that went into its seasoning can be seen in some old barns whose unpainted surfaces are still free from rot while most of the nails that held them together are rusted out. The longevity of the wood was due to the careful selection of the kind of wood chosen for the particular job, consideration of grain characteristics when the wood was sawed, and the means used to season the raw timber.

Although many of the techniques used to season wood a century or two ago may seem like legends or old wives' tales, the fact is that the results were much better than what we achieve with today's kiln-dried process. Some old carpenters believed that logs should be thoroughly soaked for days or weeks in water, then left to dry in a vertical position. Others let the wood dry naturally by girdling the

Barns bark around the trunk of a tree, letting the tree die, and felling it several months or a year later. By that time the wood had pretty much dried out naturally and thoroughly.

A painted barn is usually indicative of later nineteenth-century construction. As the knowledge of paint-making developed, less attention was paid to seasoning. The paints were produced by the individual farmer from common materials which were either close at hand or available cheaply. The paint materials were skim milk, red iron oxide, and lime. These ingredients, with the addition of linseed oil, which was found to give better penetration, made for the durable, colorful, red-toned finish we associate with New England barn architecture.

Patterns and shading of slowly weathering wood provide the interest in this barn.

Unusual curved-spoke round window in this mid-nineteenth-century barn in Tyringham, Massachusetts, required high degree of craftsmanship.

Star-shaped openings in the loft are not uncommon in southeastern New Hampshire barns.

There is no problem dating this New Hampshire barn. Cupola is exceptionally large for this area.

A small barn nestles into a Vermont hillside, where it becomes an unobtrusive part of the landscape.

Now empty, great barn was once the hub of a prosperous Cheshire, Connecticut, farm.

This drawing of a barn in Middlefield, Connecticut, was originally published in 1881. Barn in preceding photograph incorporates much of the architecture and was erected less than fifteen miles away.

Huge five-story barn in Roxbury, Connecticut, is unusual in that it was built for a dairy herd as late as 1940. It now houses chickens.

40

Well-lit three-story hayloft of working dairy barn on outskirts of Keene, New Hampshire.

Two examples in New Hampshire of barns connected to living quarters. This design precluded the necessity of going out in bad weather to tend the livestock.

Leaning cupola and strong diagonal lines of this late nineteenth-century barn keep the eye busy.

Empty silos will eventually be torn down. Farm has not been worked in twenty years.

This painted barn shows signs of weathering in the severe New England winter.

The message is clear even if the symbol is upside down.

The owners of this barn went to some trouble to express their message.

Flat-roofed barns are unusual in New England because of stress imposed by heavy snow loads.

Stone barn in Tyringham, Massachusetts, was not built for livestock but as a secure, even-temperatured place to store fruit, vegetables, and other perishables.

Detail of door of stone barn in preceding photograph. Wrought-iron hinge is part of original 150-year-old building while wooden door is a recent restoration.

Stonework portion of original early nineteenth-century barn was used to construct simple shed barn one hundred years later.

Fairly recent milk house was built from the most available material—native fieldstone.

Where the skilled labor could be obtained, strong, economical barns were built from the stone collected during the clearing of the fields.

CHAPTER 3

Transition from General to Specialized Barns

Most of the eighteenth- and early nineteenth-century barns found in New England were really multipurpose structures. This is quite different from our more recent barns, which are designed for one particular function such as dairying, curing tobacco, raising poultry, or storing a specialized crop such as potatoes or fruit. Barns built more than one hundred years ago were meant to shelter livestock, store grain and fodder, and protect carriages and wagons. It appears that some of the old barns are still performing the function of a garage, but instead of housing oxen, horses, and a buggy, today one finds the tractor, the pickup, and the station wagon.

The main barn floor, either at ground level in single-story barns or on the floor above the livestock in two- or three-level barns, was originally given over to the threshing of grain. After gathering, the grain sheaves were spread out on a large central open space on the barn floor. Then the farmer and his helpers would beat the stalks of grain with a flail to crush the kernels and break them away from the straw. The flail was a wooden pole with another straight wooden arm (called a swingle) attached to it with a leather thong. The crushed grain would then be gathered in preparation for winnowing and the straw collected and stored for use as animal bedding.

Winnowing the grain entailed separating the kernels of grain from the husks or chaff. On a windy day previously threshed grain was swept into a wide shallow tray and tossed upward into the air. The wind would blow away the lighter materials, and the grain would fall back into the tray. The grains usually treated in this manner were wheat, oats, corn, and barley. Since so much labor had gone into producing the grain, farmers usually provided a separate, tightly constructed room in which the grain could be stored. This grain bin was made with a strong dry floor, plastered walls, and a secure door that could be locked. All of this was to prevent theft, discourage rats or mice, and prevent rot caused by dampness.

This threshing area, including the straw storage mows on each side of it and the grain bin, was the most important part of the early barn. At this time the requirements of the few farm animals present were provided by lean-to shelters or small sheds attached to the main barn structure. As the number of animals and their employment in farm tasks increased, more attention and space were given to their welfare.

The height of the barn was raised to give over the first floor to livestock and the floor above for threshing and storage. The heavy farm implements such as plows, harrows, wagons, sleds, tackle, and harnesses were usually stored on the same floor as the animals. Keeping more livestock brought about some other changes in barn architecture. The most obvious of these was the modification of roof design.

In order to be able to store larger quantities of hay, the traditional pitched roof gave way to the gambrel. A gambrel roof consists of four planes rather than two. The two planes at the top are fairly flat with very little pitch, whereas the sides are long and steep. This provided a great deal of additional space under the eaves. Also, it was possible for a man to walk upright under any part of the roof. Another benefit of this roof design was that the main supports were located near the sides of the eaves leaving the center area unobstructed.

Although as many functions as possible were incorporated into a farmer's main barn, his farm continued to grow, and eventually more space was needed. Most farmers solved this problem simply by putting up additional buildings and sheds as they were needed. As the number of these outbuildings proliferated, some farms began to resemble small villages. Lean-tos were appended to barns; corncribs and ice, chicken, and smoke houses appeared. In the colder parts of New England, especially north of Massachusetts, these buildings, cropping up like afterthoughts, were joined one to another. They were built between the house and the main barn so that the farmers could perform their chores in any of the buildings without going outdoors in bad weather.

One of the most ambitious innovations in American barn design was created by the Shakers at their community in Hancock, Massachusetts. The Shakers, an austere, celibate religious group, were dedicated to excellence in all their endeavors. Their pride in workmanship and productivity was reflected in their efforts to improve existing farming methods. In 1826 the Shakers at Hancock built a huge round stone barn. This barn, 270 feet in circumference and with stone walls up to 3½ feet thick and 21 feet high, was planned to replace several outmoded barns the prospering community had already outgrown.

The Hancock barn was designed to house fifty-two head of cattle in a circular arrangement on the bottom floor around a central hay-mow. The mow was supplied from the floor above by a ramp fifteen feet wide, around which wagons could be driven to deliver the hay to the mow. This circular driveway inside the barn was conceived to serve also as a threshing floor, but the Shakers soon found that it interfered with the dairying operation.

The barn burned in 1864 and was rebuilt in 1865 with several improvements and modifications. The space below the cattle was excavated to serve as a manure pit large enough to drive a wagon through to collect the manure dropped down into it through trap doors above. The original pointed conical roof was modified into the almost flat twelve-windowed clerestory plus the large cupola we see in the restored model today. These changes provided more light to the mow area and much better ventilation throughout.

Although a few round barns had been built in America prior to 1826, the Shaker round barn was unique for its size, its cost (about ten thousand dollars), and the efficient arrangement of all of its functions. Other farmers soon copied the Shaker version, and its influence can be seen in smaller surviving examples in New England and in the midwestern plains states. Most of the adaptations were constructed with wood framing rather than stone and the plan modified into a sixteen-sided structure. In *Barn Plans and Outbuildings* Halsted accounts for the change as follows: "There is no economy in building a strictly round barn, as curved walls, sills, cornice and roofing are very expensive and offset the trifling gain in floor space." The round plan evolved into an octagonal shape, and some of these barns are still standing.

Fortunately, the great Shaker round stone barn can be seen today. It was completely and expensively restored in 1968 and is the focal point of the Hancock Shaker Community Preservation. It was a landmark in American barn architecture and led to the erection of the larger, more specialized farming factories we associate with our present agricultural methods.

Another great Shaker barn is still standing a few miles across the Massachusetts border from Hancock at the site of the New

Lebanon, New York, Shaker community. This is a five-story stone barn about as long as a football field. The New (later changed to Mount) Lebanon Shakers became one of the largest Shaker communities, and the immense barn was a necessity. Without a great deal of repair or restoration the barn still stands as evidence of the care and integrity that went into its building. However, the barn, now a part of a private school that purchased the Shaker holdings at Mount Lebanon, will require the same expensive restoration given to the round barn at Hancock if it is to survive.

The advantages of using stone in the construction of the foundation or superstructure of a New England barn are obvious. The material was abundant, cost nothing, was extremely durable, and required little maintenance. It did not need to be painted, would not rot, and was impervious to the weather. One factor limiting its more extensive use in barn or house design was the relative scarcity of laborers skilled in stonework. Also, construction with stone was slower than with timber. The problem of providing scaffolding as the work progressed higher and higher and the lifting of heavy stones were great burdens. As clever as the Shakers were in the working of wood and metal, the builders of the Hancock round barn found it necessary to hire expensive masons from the "outside world."

Apparently, expediency and a lack of heritage of building with stone dictated the more prevalent wooden barn construction in New England. The Germans in Pennsylvania with a background in masonry built fortresslike stone barns two hundred years ago that still stand except for those that have been deliberately destroyed. In New England we find that the relatively few barns and houses made of stone are rarely more than one story high.

As farming in New England progressed into the nineteenth century, many farmers found it to their advantage to specialize in producing a single crop for its cash value. In areas where it was found that the terrain was too hilly and rocky or the growing season too short to raise corn or other grains profitably, landowners turned to dairy farming. Vermont, for instance, converted so thoroughly to dairying that for a long time it was referred to as the state with more cows than people.

Prior to 1850 most farmers kept only enough cows to supply milk for their own consumption or to make less perishable butter and cheese. To make dairy farming an economically feasible venture required a fairly large-sized herd and a big enough barn to shelter it and facilitate the milking operation. This spurred the design and building of larger barns where the production, handling, and storage of bulk quantities of milk could be carried out with better efficiency.

Agricultural schools at state colleges sprang up and devoted themselves to studying improvements in barn design and farming methods. Among the developments to come from this research were barn ventilation and sanitation. Air shafts were introduced that ran the full height of the barn and terminated in louvered cupolas on the roof. In some barns these ventilating shafts also served as chutes for the delivery of fodder from the hayloft to the cattle on the floor below. Earth or wooden-plank barn floors were replaced by cement, which was more durable and far easier to clean.

With increased herd size came the necessity of enlarging the space allotted for the storage of hay and other animal fodder. Roofs were raised and enlarged with dormers or ballooned with gambrels as much as possible. When that space became inadequate, silos were built. Silos, in the tall round form we see today, were a fairly late development in American barn construction, first appearing in the last quarter of the nineteenth century. Those made of wood were unique in their construction in that they were not built around a frame but were merely a shell of boards held together by iron bands, very much like a barrel. The reasons we do not see more stone silos in New England dating from this period is that a silo was usually considered a temporary structure, and the time and cost of erecting a permanent one did not seem justified.

The area extending for several miles on each side of the Connecticut River from Hartford north into Massachusetts is the heart of the shade-grown, broadleaf tobacco industry. For years it was recognized that these few square miles of flat, well-drained, red-clay-like soil and the right amount of rainfall and sunshine grew the best cigar-wrapper tobacco in the world. Although the raising of this fine tobacco involves a huge amount of labor and risk, it always commanded a premium price, and great fortunes were made from its cultivation.

For the tobacco to be grown in shade, row after row of wooden poles must be sunk in the ground and acres of netting, resembling cheesecloth, stretched over them. During the growing season the delicate plants are susceptible to exotic insects and fungi, and a sudden summer thunderstorm accompanied by hail can wipe out an entire season's crop. After the tobacco is harvested, the leaves must be slowly dried to the proper degree so that they are not brittle and will conform to the filler when they are rolled into cigars.

To accomplish this slow drying, a type of barn was developed that appears to be indigenous only to this locality. The main considerations in building a Connecticut Valley tobacco barn were size, economy, and ventilation. It required a barn thirty by a hundred feet, covering roughly one-tenth of an acre, to dry the tobacco grown on three acres of land. Hundreds of such barns were built, varying very little except in size and method of ventilation. The height of a typical tobacco barn was twenty feet to the eaves, with the bents or frame sections spaced about fifteen feet apart. Across the width of the barn four tiers of cross braces were fastened. The poles upon which the tobacco was hung were laid the length of the barn and supported by the cross members. Overhead clearance to the first tier was usually at least seven feet so that wagons could be driven into the barn from the fields.

Ventilation was achieved by hinging alternate vertical boards of siding near the top so that they swung out about two feet at the bottom. Variations on this plan came later with horizontal siding that could be opened like a louvered door a section at a time by raising one vertical tie-piece. Earlier tobacco barns had no provision for venting near the peak of the roof; later ones show a raised section running the length of the roof at the peak like a long, flat cupola.

In the past twenty years the Connecticut shade-grown tobacco industry has shrunk considerably. The chief factor contributing to its lessened importance was the development of homogenized tobacco cigar wrapper. In this process lower-grade tobacco is pulverized and rolled into sheets like paper. Although it does not have all of the slow, even-burning, aromatic properties of the shade-grown leaf, it is considerably cheaper and better adapted to automated cigar-making machinery. This loss of industry, in addition to rising land values, has accelerated the destruction of Connecticut tobacco barns. Industry has found the acres of flat, unobstructed tobacco fields ideal for building sprawling one-story factories and warehouses, and developers seek it out for shopping centers and housing tracts. As valuable as the tobacco crop once was, the land is now worth more for what can be built on it than for what it can grow.

The Connecticut tobacco barns were built to be strictly functional, and very little attention to detail and finish went into their construction. Many timbers can be found in them with the bark still on, and the lumber and hardware were of a very rough grade. Since these barns were never painted, the long flat siding has weathered beautifully. Barns fifty years and older have been stripped at such a furious rate that probably fewer than one hundred barns of that vintage still stand.

Other specialized barns and farm buildings found in New England are potato barns, corncribs, icehouses, springhouses, and smoke-houses. The potato barns, found mostly in Maine and Rhode Island, were merely huge storage sheds similar to the tobacco barns but built taller, not as long, and with very little ventilation. Their only purpose was to protect the crop from spoilage prior to shipment.

Corncribs were once found on nearly every farm that raised corn for feeding livestock. The ears of corn contain a great deal of moisture and must be dried thoroughly before they can be fed to the animals. Rats and mice were the farmer's special enemy in the storing of corn, and a building had to be designed that allowed ventilation but would not permit access to the rodents.

This was accomplished by building the corncribs on posts two or three feet above the ground. The posts were covered with inverted tin pans that did not allow the rats to climb the posts. The floor of the corncrib was covered with boards laid an inch to an inch and a half apart to permit air to enter freely. A typical corncrib can be recognized by its sidewalls, which slant outward from the bottom to the eaves, giving it a V-shaped profile. The corncrib is generally a small building from six to eight feet wide and ten to twenty feet long. Early farmers preferred to build several small corncribs rather than one large one because the smaller ones were thought to do a better job.

Icehouses did not become common farm buildings until well into the nineteenth century. By that time it was recognized that ice, which could be conveniently harvested at no cost except for labor, would prevent expensive spoilage of meat and dairy products. Nearly every farm had access to a nearby pond or lake from which the ice could be sawed and hauled on sleds to the icehouse.

The structural considerations in building an efficient icehouse were outlined in the 1881 book *Barn Plans and Outbuildings*:

> There are some general principles to be observed in the proper construction of any kind of ice house, and all else is of secondary importance. There must be perfect drainage beneath, ample ventilation and perfect dryness above, and sufficient non-conducting material for packing below, above and around the ice, by which its low temperature may be preserved.

The recommended packing, or insulation, was sawdust, charcoal powder, straw, or marsh hay.

Usually the icehouse was sunk a foot or two below the ground level in dry, porous soil and then built up with inner and outer walls between which the insulation was packed. The recommended roof

59

had broad, overhanging eaves to shade the walls as much as possible. Some icehouses were built so that the ice could be stored above an open storage space. This type required much stronger walls to support the weight of the ice and were generally made of stone or brick. Except for a ventilator at the top of the roof, extreme care had to be taken to make the ice storage space both airtight and watertight. Any drafts capable of passing through the floor would melt away the ice in a very short time.

Modern refrigeration methods have made the icehouse obsolete, and very few remain now. This is true also of the springhouse, a building formerly needed on any dairy farm. In a springhouse shallow ten-quart pans of fresh milk were placed to cool in wide water troughs arranged around three sides of the inside of the springhouse. These troughs were fed with water piped from a nearby cool spring. Either they were sunk below floor level, or if the spring was elevated, they were set up on raised benches.

Springhouses had to be well insulated and required a much higher level of interior finish than an icehouse. Floors were stone or cement, and walls were plastered and whitewashed. This was done to promote a clean, cool environment from which insects and other pests could be excluded. One hundred square feet of trough area could be included in a springhouse twelve feet wide and twenty-four feet long. This was large enough to service a herd of twenty cows.

Exposing meat to woodsmoke is a primitive method of preservation that has been practiced almost as long as we have recorded history. The naturally cured, slowly smoked ham is now a premium-priced delicacy which was once more common than fresh meat. Every farm needed a smokehouse, and they were built, as were all early farm buildings, as simple and functional as possible. Part or, ideally, most of a smokehouse was built of stone or brick to contain the fire and ashes. The meat was hung as far as possible away from the fire, as it is the smoke, not the heat, that accomplishes the curing or preservative process.

The smokehouse could be of any size—from a barrel to a barn—that could be shut up tight and filled with smoke. Unless it was built entirely of brick with a curved dome-topped roof, it is not very likely that an ordinary smokehouse would be distinguishable from the half-dozen or so miscellaneous outbuildings on the average farm.

Most of the small farm buildings are now gone or are in an advanced stage of decay. They were not built like the old barns, whose heavy mortised beams permit them to stand a few more years until they, too, finally crumble or succumb to the developer's bulldozers.

Built in 1826, the great Shaker round barn in Hancock, Massachusetts, is 90 feet in diameter, four stories high, and with stone walls up to 3½ feet thick. This 1968 restoration follows the design of the barn as it was reconstructed by the Shakers in 1865 after a disastrous fire in 1864.

Interior view of the Shaker round barn showing the elaborate network of rafters required for roof. Structure in center is ventilating shaft extending from barn floor to cupola.

View through a window in Shaker round barn shows strength and thickness of masonry construction.

Round design of the Shaker barn influenced agricultural architecture in the United States. This octagon-shaped barn in Woodbury, Connecticut, is a more easily constructed adaptation of a circular plan.

This barn was one of the largest ever constructed in this country. Built by the Shakers in the 1860's, it was located a few miles west of Pittsfield, Massachusetts, in New Lebanon, New York. It was almost three hundred feet long, five stories high, and built completely of stone. Some idea of its size can be realized from the cupola, which was the size of a small cottage. This barn burned in September, 1972, and there is little hope that it will ever be restored. All that now remains is the stone shell seen below.

Storage barn and wagon shed at the rear of the large stone Shaker barn at New Lebanon, New York. Shape of cupola is peculiar to Shakers.

Modern barns are less pleasing to the eye and do not age as gracefully as those of the past two centuries.

Heifer looks out from behind her fenced pasture.

Icehouse built by Shakers at Hancock, Massachusetts. Brick building was well insulated and finished with close-fitting doors and slate roof.

A triple set of windows was employed in the icehouse at Hancock Shaker village to provide insulation while admitting light to the storage room.

Corncribs were built two or three feet above the ground to protect them from rats and mice. Narrow spaces between siding slats facilitated the drying process. Tapered shape of sides is distinctive feature of New England cribs.

Victorian carriage houses allowed builders freedom for more ornate barn design.

73

Three long Connecticut tobacco barns situated in the middle of the netting-covered fields.

Tobacco growing under the netting in Windsor Locks, Connecticut. In the rear is tremendous tobacco barn.

The plowed and fertilized tobacco fields, with the shade netting in place, await
the late-spring planting.

Typical barn used for drying Connecticut Valley shade-grown broadleaf tobacco, which provides world's best cigar wrappers. The barn is ventilated by hinging every third siding board so that it can be swung out at the bottom and still protect the tobacco from rain. Air escapes at the roof through vents running the length of the peak.

Alternate method of tobacco barn ventilation is provided by horizontally applied siding that can be opened like louvers. By lifting the upright boards that are connected by hinges to sections of the siding, air is admitted along the full length of the barn.

The desirable siding has already been stripped from this tobacco barn, exposing the interior lattice needed to support the rows of poles upon which the tobacco was hung to dry.

In its last days with only the bents and roof still standing, this old Connecticut tobacco barn captures the eye with the honest lines of its basic structure.

A flock of pigeons finds a home in an abandoned tobacco barn.

CHAPTER 4

Finding a Barn to Remodel

THERE must be a kind of innate recognition of some of the architectural virtues of New England barns. The features of line, shape, and grace that distinguish the typical old barns have been reflected in the design of many private dwellings for over two hundred years. The most distinctive New England barn shape is the saltbox with its short steep roof in front and long sloping roof in the rear. In some cases the built-out portion in the rear may have come about through an addition of a lean-to to an original boxlike structure. But it was not long before American builders incorporated its advantages into the original plans for their barns and houses.

Typically, the long low roof in the rear faced to the north. This made the ceiling height of rooms in that part of the structure lower and easier to heat. Also, snow would remain on that section longer and act as additional insulation. The taller facade in front faced south so that it could be heated by the sun. Houses built in the saltbox style became ubiquitous in New England and are still being built today.

Where more interior space was desired, the gambrel roof was employed to enlarge the rooms on the upper floor. This style permitted higher ceilings and more floor space unobstructed by interior supports and bracing. The gambrel roof is usually associated with the early Dutch settlers and seems to have spread to New England from New York and the Hudson River valley.

Although some of the superficial aspects of barn design are being   81 perpetuated in new home construction, the more important features are being sacrificed. Mostly because of cost considerations we are losing the sense of great interior space and the feeling of warmth and solidity reflected in the massive handcrafted structural members. Unless one is able to commit unlimited funds to incorporating these elements in a new home, it is generally less expensive and more satisfying to remodel an old barn.

To judge from the number of barns that have been resurrected, reconstructed, and remodeled into permanent and vacation dwellings, the project has wide appeal. There are people willing to devote the time, labor, money, and patience to create a unique home from a structure that might have either become a picturesque ruin or disappeared forever. Regardless of the frustrations, unexpected problems, and a sense of never quite being finished, few would have opted for a new prefab or older traditional house if they had it to do over.

The principal attraction in converting an old barn into a home is the great amount of unencumbered space. Great freedom is permitted in working out a floor plan and the placement of rooms. Aside from a few upright supporting columns, there are no bearing walls to contend with. Interior walls have to be made only sturdy enough to partition the rooms, not to support an upper floor. This also enhances the flexibility of interior design.

After one has determined that he will be content only with the type of home that can be made from a barn, the next step is to find a suitable barn for the purpose. One may already be familiar with a suitable location with a potentially habitable barn still standing on it. Or one may have to spend weekends becoming familiar with an area by driving around it, exploring back roads and country lanes away from the superhighways.

Your prospecting in this manner might be rewarded by coming upon the ideal situation and being able to approach the owner directly. More likely, however, it would be better to contact a reputable agent specializing in farm realty. If you are timorous about approaching the man behind the first real-estate shingle you come to, check with an officer of one of the local banks. He will be happy to recommend several reliable people in that field and might also anticipate handling the financing in case you should buy in that market.

There are a number of important points to bear in mind when looking for a barn or a piece of country real estate. You must be sure that the property is served by electric and telephone lines; if it is not, can these be brought in by the utility companies at little or no cost to you? Next, you must be assured that a well can be drilled to provide an adequate amount of water without going so deep as to make it prohibitively expensive. One other factor that should be remembered is that of drainage. You will not find an old barn with a fully operative septic system. You will be obliged to install a new septic tank and leaching field. This would be the case in any construction where there is no access to a municipal sewer line, but it is still prudent to be aware of these additional items of expense.

It is possible that a barn you select will have to be moved to another site. This has been done many times before and presents no special problems for an experienced contractor. In some cases it may be possible to dismantle a barn carefully, discarding what cannot be used and reassembling the essential elements at a new location. The main items one should attempt to preserve are the size, form, and framework of the old barn. No barn is worth the effort of restoration if its skeleton of vertical posts and horizontal crossbeams has deteriorated past the point of salvage. With a sound frame one can eventually realize results that will be worth the effort.

A fairly high percentage of those who undertake barn-remodeling plan to do a great deal of the work themselves. For some it has been a husband-and-wife or family weekend project for years. Obviously, a lot of money can be saved in this way, and although progress may be slow, there is a much deeper sense of personal accomplishment when the job is finished. Unless one is quite experienced or technically competent, mechanical systems such as plumbing, heating, and electrical work should be contracted to professionals. Although some localities still permit an owner to do whatever he wishes on his own property, the adoption of building codes even in rural areas may require the use of licensed plumbers and electricians.

The least expensive approach to the actual construction is to find a well-regarded local carpenter who will undertake overall supervision of the job for an hourly rate plus a reasonable fee. This is on the assumption that he is experienced in this kind of work and you are not employing an architect. On the other hand, if you are unable to envision the finished product or if the quality of the available labor is not first-rate, an architect's planning and supervision will be essential.

The major structural details that must be considered before the work can progress very far are exterior siding, roof, windows, and heating. In some cases a barn is found where the siding is in good enough condition to be left as is, with perhaps a small amount of repair or replacement of worn or missing boards or shingles. If not, it may be practical to strip salvageable siding from the barn to be used later for interior paneling. In that case the exterior will need to be resided with material in harmony with the period in which the barn was originally built. This could be boards taken from other buildings on the property or bought from someone who is dismantling an old barn nearby. The most satisfactory new material for siding appears to be plain wooden shingles, which in time will weather to a pleasing grayish patina.

Just about every old barn will require a new roof to make the building habitable. The most authentic-looking restoration of a roof can be made by using wooden shingles. This is a fairly costly method, and most owners will apply asphalt shingles in order to save money. In doing this it is wise to avoid a color or pattern that will conflict with the antique ambience you are trying to achieve.

Providing windows for a barn entails making the most drastic modification in the external appearance of the building. The few windows that may be found in an old barn will usually not be suitable for housing purposes. They are likely to be small and fixed in a way that does not permit enough ventilation. Normally, they are replaced by larger, multi-paned double-hung or casement types that are in keeping with the early rustic theme. In the less exposed part of the barn at the back and away from traffic many owners install large glass walls and sliding glass doors. This does not alter the traditional front of the building while opening up the interior to admit more light and air.

Some of the most dramatic restorations involve the creative use and placement of new windows. Entire sidewalls have been replaced with glass from the bottom sill to roof peak with startlingly beautiful results. It is best to try to work with commercially available windows made at a mill in stock sizes. There is a great variety of sizes and styles from which to choose, and they are less expensive than custom-made units would be.

How elaborate a heating system you decide to put into a barn dwelling depends upon whether it is contemplated as a year-round home or merely for summer occupancy. In the latter case a fireplace may be all you will need for chilly evenings. To make it habitable in all seasons, however, heating will prove to be a major problem. The simplest solution in terms of construction and installation cost is

electrical heating. It can be installed quickly and offers a lot of flexibility, as the heating units can be placed wherever they are needed.
The disadvantages of electric heat are its high operating cost and inefficient heating of large spaces with high ceilings.

More economical heating can be obtained through the installation of an oil-fired hot-air furnace and associated ductwork. Such a furnace can be placed in a basement if there is one or in a small shed or enclosure attached to the building. Hot-air heat will provide fast warming and relatively low-cost operation.

If one plans to add a complete heating system to a remodeled barn, it will be necessary to insulate the building as thoroughly as possible. Conventional fiberglass and rock-wool blankets can be placed between the wall studs while they are exposed and before the interior paneling has been put up. In situations where the studding is already enclosed, several types of insulation can be poured or blown into the spaces between the inner and outer walls from openings under the eaves. A fairly new method of placing insulation on the inside of existing walls involves the use of a polyurethane foam. This compound is sprayed into the open spaces between the studs by injecting under pressure a liquid chemical which foams as it is being ejected from the nozzle. After a short time the foam hardens and becomes a rigid mass sealing every crack and opening. As this material will flow freely into any size or shape of space into which it is introduced, it should not be used unless it can be confined to the space where it is required.

Some of the arguments that may dissuade one from undertaking the remodeling of a barn are that the building will always retain a barn odor; that it will be impossible to rid the premises of rats, mice, and other small animals; and that nothing can be made truly level and plumb except at great expense. Experience has proved that a barn odor does not linger after the place has been cleaned, new lumber installed, and paint or stain applied. Also, while the initial stages of construction are under way, the building is open to a degree that permits excellent airing.

Rodents and other animal pests will not remain once their food supply is gone. They have no sentiment for surroundings and will be present only as long as grain or other food can be found. Field mice and squirrels will try to find a warm place in any country home, but they can be excluded by tight construction and by not leaving doors or windows open for their entrance.

There is no reason to expect that every part of a barn that has been standing one hundred years or more will have remained perfectly level or perpendicular. The chances are that it was not built that way in the first place. Many contractors will be reluctant to tackle this kind of work without trying to convince the owner that before reconstruction can proceed, everything must be trued up. This is the way they are accustomed to work on new construction, and their biases can carry over into a remodeling job.

Unless you can find a carpenter who is willing to work with old material and not try to level up one end of the floor by raising it a degree or two, you will probably have to spend a lot of extra money or do a good deal of the work yourself. Contractors experienced in barn remodeling and who share an owner's enthusiasm in restoration will not be too finicky over minor details. They will endeavor to do the job well while retaining that certain unsophisticated handcrafted look you are trying to achieve.

This is accomplished by working within the original lines of the building and by preserving as many of the architectural details as possible. The most obvious elements are the old hand-hewn structural beams. These will be rough and still show the marks of the broadax which was used to shape them from the log. Smooth-sided beams cut at a sawmill are still impressive due to their size and mellowness but lack the desirable evidence of handwork. Most of the time these beams are absolutely sound, and their mortised and pegged joints have lost none of their strength and rigidity. However, if they are going to bear a lot more weight or stress than they were originally designed for, or if the joints appear to have some looseness or play, it will be necessary to reinforce them. This is usually done by placing steel plates over the joints and bolting them into the beams. A better method, in aesthetic terms, is to install a diagonal wooden brace at the point where the upright and horizontal beams are joined.

Other features in an old barn that would be worth some effort to keep would be original flooring, siding, and perhaps an unusual window or a huge stone doorsill. They may not be able to be used exactly where they are found, but with proper thought and planning their incorporation will enhance the appearance of the finished reconstruction.

Christmas-card scenes like this one are found during a winter's drive in rural New England.

This farmer appears to have only recently made the transition from horses to tractors.

Hay laid up in the barn mow and waiting for winter.

Saltbox-shape barn has wagon shed at rear.

Saltbox house built in 1789 is only slightly modified version of barn design.

Modern barn with gambrel roof dominates hilltop on farm of affluent owner.

Recently built home with gambrel roof has typical barn look.

Windmills used to pump water for cattle were once much more numerous in the grazing meadows of New England.

The grain mill was an important part of early American agriculture. This is upper millstone with the grooving and lands to provide particular type of grind. Bottom stone was flat. On view at Bennington Museum in Vermont.

Upright stone posts were used as early farm boundary markers. This one has been drilled through to make a sturdy gatepost.

95

Cupolas with their weather vanes and lightning rods were a part of a barn where the builder could exercise his imagination and creativity, as shown in the examples here through page 103. Although some cupolas were purely utilitarian, others evidenced elaborate scrollwork and design.

Early agricultural implements were often made by the man who had to use them. This hayfork was made from a single piece of applewood. (*Coe Collection*)

Flail used to thresh grain consisted of a long wooden handle joined to the shorter "swingle" by a leather binding. (*Coe Collection*)

Several early ax heads including, at right, the broadax used to hew square timbers from the fallen log. At upper left is the head of a small adze used for rough trimming. (*Mattatuck Museum Collection*)

Half broadax, half hatchet, this tool performed dozens of jobs around the farm. (*Mattatuck Museum Collection*)

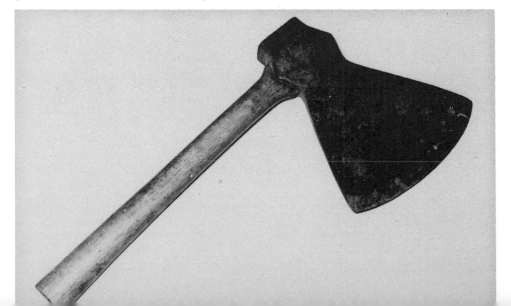

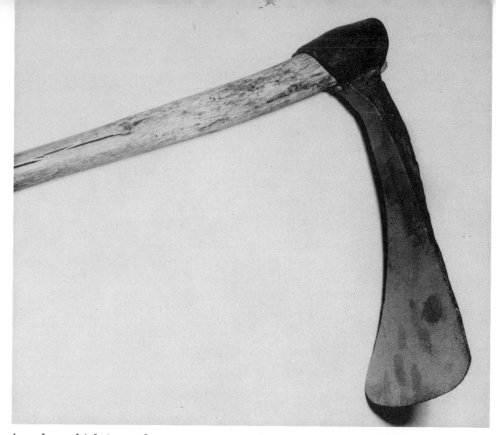

An adze, which is used to secure a smoother trim of hewn timbers. (*Mattatuck Museum Collection*)

Shingles and rough clapboards were made with this tool called a froe. Held with the wooden handle upright, the slightly dull blade was placed on top of a section of log and the end of the blade struck with a wooden mallet or maul. This split the log into as thick or thin sections as desired. (*Mattatuck Museum Collection*)

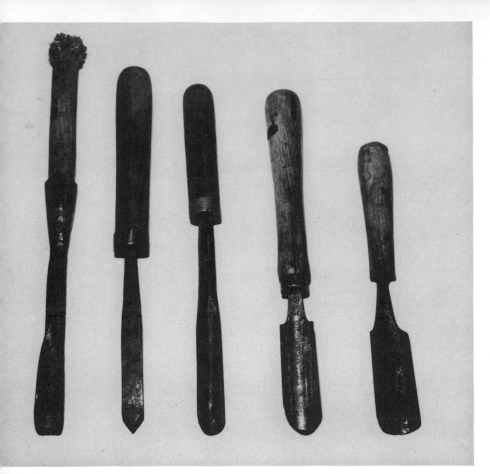

Specialized chisels were employed in fashioning
the mortises and tenons for the fitting of structural beams. (*Mattatuck Museum Collection*)

Auger used to make holes in beams through
which wooden pegs were driven to fasten the
joints. (*Coe Collection*)

108

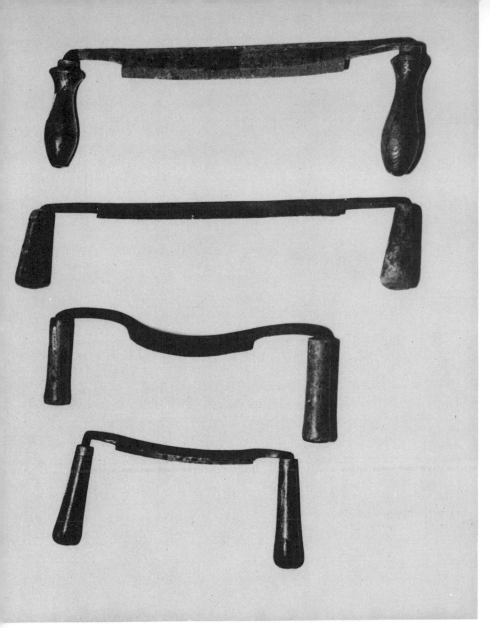

The drawknife was a rudimentary type of plane. It was drawn across work toward the operator. Second tool from bottom has curved profile and could be used to make barrel staves. (*Mattatuck Museum Collection*)

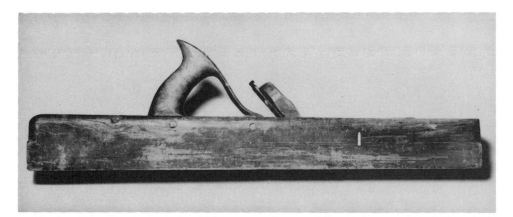

Wood plane of mid-nineteenth century. Blade was secured by wooden wedge driven firmly between blade and block. (*Mattatuck Museum Collection*)

109

Six early building squares. Steel square at top has crudely etched inch markings
and divisions. (*Mattatuck Museum Collection*)

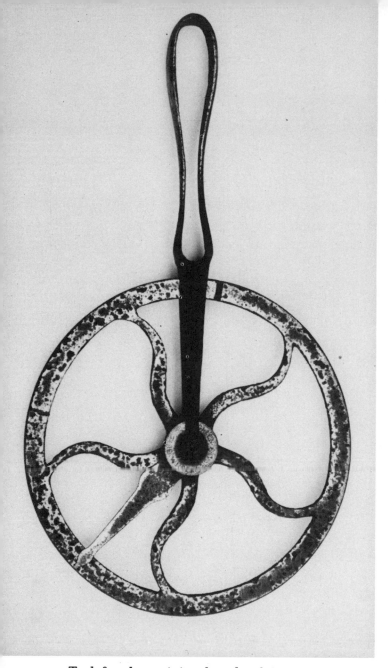

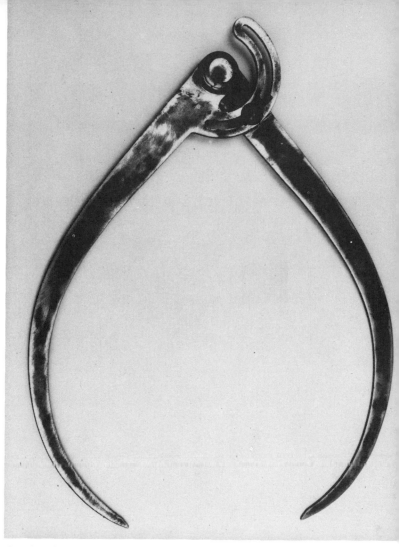

Steel caliper with wide opening for sizing beams to uniform thickness. (*Coe Collection*)

Tool for determining length of iron wagon tire. Wheel was run around outer circumference of wagon wheel, and the number of rotations noted. By repeating the process along a strip of iron the tire could be cut to the right length. (*Coe Collection*)

This nasty-looking tool is a "sugar devil." It was used to loosen sugar after it had hardened in the barrel. (*Mattatuck Museum Collection*)

Circular saw was useful in many ways around the farm.

This six-foot saw was used to cut blocks of ice from frozen lakes and ponds. (*Coe Collection*)

Old horse-drawn plows and rakes lie unused in storage area under this New England barn.

Construction of bents or preassembled frame sections can be seen in this photograph of a barn in Northfield, Connecticut, shortly before it was completely torn down.

Detail showing beams and braces mortised into each other and secured by oak pegs. This part of the barn is still in good condition while siding has all but rotted away.

End bent is all that is still standing of a barn in Moretown, Vermont. Unhewn cross timbers were inserted after bent was erected to add support for siding. Shed at left was later construction.

Another view of mortise and tenon construction in corner upright of barn. Marks of broadax are still evident on the timbers.

Barn siding patched with scrap pieces from the sawmill.

Detail of floor construction in old barn. Square-timbered sill is laid over stone foundation and plain untrimmed logs laid across to support planks for floor.

120

Detail of inside beam showing how hardwood pegs were inserted through post to make a simple, practical ladder to the hayloft above.

View of exposed structural members conveys the feeling of the strength and dignity that make an old barn so attractive.

Old wagon wheel is left to rot in field and becomes a part of the landscape.

CHAPTER 5

How Three Owners
Renovated Their Barns

IT will be instructive to examine three recent barn renovations. We will want to know what each owner started with, what his objectives were, and how well he succeeded in meeting them.

The first example we shall deal with is actually two barns, one dating back to about the middle of the nineteenth century and a larger, attached barn built early in this century. These buildings with ten acres of land are located on a hilltop in Woodbury, Connecticut, commanding a fifty-mile view to the south, east, and west. The couple who bought this property are both artists. The husband is a painter, graphic designer, and sculptor, and his wife works with ceramics and textiles. They both needed extensive studio space to pursue their work besides living quarters for themselves and two children.

The larger, more modern building was converted into a house by partitioning the second floor into a living and dining area, kitchen, bath, and combination master bedroom and painter's studio. Bedrooms were made for the children on the third floor. The ground floor was left relatively unfinished and is used for the wife's workroom. Numerous windows were cut into this building with the bedroom-studio being furnished with a large industrial-type window to admit north light.

The full height of part of the older barn is utilized by the sculptor-husband for work on heavy, large-scale wood and metal pieces. This area is lighted by four large multi-paned windows. The rest of this building is a woodworking shop, where much of the carpentry needed to remodel both buildings was done.

On the exterior both barns had new shingles applied and were reroofed. New gutters and leaders were also installed. A large sun deck extends almost the full length of both buildings. Evergreen shrubs were planted along this terrace to soften the lines and assist in the landscaping effort.

The most striking room in the residential wing is the master bedroom. Extravagant use of the space available was made by extending the room the entire depth of the building front to back with a thirteen-foot-high ceiling. A raised gallery and bookcases were built along the inner wall, which furnishes excellent storage space. The room is painted white, including the floor, which is made of four-by-eight-foot plywood sheets. This adds to the feeling of spaciousness and serves as a proper background for the paintings.

All of the construction was done by the owner except for the plumbing, heating, and roofing, which were contracted. Working alone or with his wife, he did all the carpentry and masonry and installed the complete wiring system. Prior to this undertaking he had devoted 350 to 400 hours in designing and helping to build a studio for a local fellow artist. When that project was finished, his friend spent an equal amount of time helping with the heavier, more complicated work on his barn. This included jacking up the older barn

to construct a new foundation, installing windows, laying floors, and taking out or moving beams. This sharing of work is reminiscent of the old-time barn-raisings, where friends and neighbors would assist one another by contributing their labor to help build a new barn.

It has taken this couple seven years to accomplish what they have. Since they are both employed as full-time art instructors, they could work only as time and the availability of money permitted. The result of their labor is a comfortable home and wonderful space in which to pursue their individual talents. They also have a building in which every part reflects their own personal character, ideas, work, and love.

There seems to be a common characteristic among the owners of remodeled barn dwellings. It is a single-minded devotion to the project, whether they are doing the work themselves or are contracting all the work to someone else. They are willing to contribute a great amount of time if they have it, labor if they can do it, and money if they can afford it.

Resurrecting a 150-year-old barn in Roxbury, Connecticut, into a unique, luxurious weekend retreat was the enterprise of a New York actor who specializes in television commercials. When he bought the property four years ago, it included a large farmhouse built in the early nineteenth century. Instead of fixing the house and letting the barns disintegrate, he decided to make his home in the biggest barn and rent the house to an artist friend.

Since his career did not permit him the time to supervise the renovation personally, he engaged a local contractor who specialized in the restoration of old structures. The barn they started with was structurally sound, with a decent roof, and since the farm had been worked up until the time he bought it, the building was supplied with electricity and water. The first problem in making the barn habitable was to find a way to weatherproof it. The building was merely a shell with one layer of decaying siding nailed to the frame. Ordinarily, the approach to this would be to lay building paper on the inside of the walls, put up studs, place insulation between the studs, and then cover the walls and ceiling with plywood paneling or better still, old barn siding. This is an expensive undertaking, to say the least.

Fortunately, a recent technical innovation solved both the aesthetic and the financial problems. The contractor was approached by two young men who wanted to experiment with a sprayed-on polyurethane foam insulation. This is a material that is being used extensively in the manufacture of thin-walled refrigerators and freezers, so there was no doubt about its insulating properties. What had to be determined was how well it would adhere to the old wooden surface and whether it would take a coat of paint.

A small area was treated with satisfactory results, and a price of fifteen hundred dollars was agreed upon for spraying all the inner surfaces of the thirty-by-fifty-foot building. This included the walls, the underside of the roof, and underneath the flooring. (The floor was the ceiling of an old cow stable below.)

The foam filled and sealed the spaces between the old boards perfectly, and in places where the openings were several inches wide some of it oozed out and ran down the side of the barn. When dry, the natural color of the now rigid foam is a light beige, which darkens gradually into brown from exposure to sunlight.

The sprayed areas were then painted a flat white, leaving the beams and rafters exposed and thereby accentuating the structural elements of the barn. The painted foam resembles stucco, and its texture, which in some places follows the contours of the boards it covers, lends character and charm to the rooms.

As testimony to the efficiency of the insulating qualities of the foam, the owner heated the barn comfortably during the first winter he spent in it with two eighty-five-dollar portable heaters. This is quite an accomplishment, for normally heating the high, open space of such a building is an expensive, unrewarding job. On a permanent basis, however, electric baseboard heaters are presently being installed.

The original barn had a structural feature rarely found in surviving New England barns. It was a large square silo attached to one corner in the rear of the building. Recognizing the possibilities the silo offered for privacy, the owner decided to use it for his own bath and sleeping quarters. The roof was raised several feet and large thermopane windows installed on the two sides away from the road and overlooking miles of open fields and wooded hills. This room at the top of the silo became the bedroom, and below it was built a

combination bath and dressing room. Access to the silo portion of the barn is through a door made out of a hinged section of bookcases in the living room.

The stairs in the silo connecting from the bath up to the bedroom are worth a special note. They are spiral in design and were made by a local craftsman who used old wood found in various buildings on the property. They are made as they would have been two hundred years ago—completely pegged and without nails.

Through the tasteful use of unusual windows salvaged from other old buildings the appearance of both the exterior and the interior is enhanced. A pair of four-foot round windows was installed under the eaves at each end of the main open area of the barn. They admit light where it is needed, as does the great fan-topped floor-to-ceiling window at the side of the room. The floors were discovered to be the original, wide chestnut boards that are now unobtainable at any price, and sanded and stained, they have an incomparable warmth and mellowness.

Passing the barn while driving, one would not be aware of the splendid home behind the plain front that faces the road. That is the least altered part of a renovation that conceals a large sun deck and swimming pool at the rear, discreetly screened by shrubbery and the contour of the land.

In an interview the contractor who has been in charge of this job since its beginning was congratulated on the very high level of craftsmanship evident in everything he had done. He preferred to credit one of his associates as the one responsible for the most meticulous and authentic parts of the restoration. This carpenter he acknowledged to be without equal in working with old materials and retaining original feelings.

He insisted, however, that none of his work or the results would have been possible without the complete cooperation of the owner. This statement was repeated several times during the conversation, and the word "cooperation" was interpreted to mean giving the contractor a free hand and a blank check.

Of the three converted barns we are considering the last is certainly the most formal. It is owned by a photographer who maintains an apartment in New York City and whose work has taken him all over the world. He prefers to live in his magnificent country home north of New Milford, Connecticut, on weekends and whenever he is not on an assignment.

The renovation of this barn required the most radical structural revision and the greatest amount of new or reused building materials. It was probably the setting of this barn on a wooded rise above a narrow, active stream that persuaded the owner that this was the place he wanted to live. Everything that would have to be done to make this barn into a home would eventually prove to be worth the effort and expense.

The finished result would tend to vindicate his determination and investment. Although the interior finish may seem somewhat austere, it is softened in the ground-floor living area by an enormous round rug and the graceful lines of French furniture with which the room is decorated.

The second level is certainly the more striking. The entire floor is open from floor to roof with the far wall completely replaced with glass right up to the peak. The other end of the room contains a fireplace with a raised hearth. A small curtained alcove on one side of the room serves for the bachelor sleeping quarters.

Very little remains of the old barn except for the main beams that still support the new construction. Siding was extensively replaced with vintage boards and a new roof applied. All interior wall and ceiling surfaces were covered with Sheetrock over the studs and painted white. New pine board floors were laid and varnished with a light stain. An interesting decorative, yet functional, detail is the use of part of an old barn door rolling on its original track to close off the kitchen.

The walls on both upper and lower floors facing the woods and brook have been opened up by using full-length sliding glass doors. These allow access to a balcony on the second floor and to a terrace off the ground floor. Providing enough windows for adequate interior lighting is perhaps one of the prime considerations of any barn restoration or renovation.

The homes that emerged from each of the three remodeled barns we have discussed reflect to a large degree the life-style and personal aspirations of the owners. The husband and wife who are

both artists have a comfortable home for themselves and their children plus incomparable studio space in which to pursue their individual talents. They have ample room in which to expand their living quarters and are now engaged in adding two additional bedrooms and a bathroom. The somewhat utilitarian look of the interior was necessitated by a severely limited budget, which dictated that most of the funds be allocated to purely functional construction. Austerity is avoided, however, by the carefully placed display of their own work and that of other artists. For that purpose, and for a spacious place in which to live and work and raise a family, this project must be considered a success.

At the other extreme from the barn remodeled over a period of seven years by an owner who contributed most of the labor and conserved every dollar of expense is the barn belonging to the television actor. Everything about this home gives evidence of a lavish expenditure of money controlled only by excellent taste. Great effort was made to preserve the original lines of the building and the best of the period architectural detailing while incorporating the most modern living conveniences. Experienced workmen were hired who either could work with the materials at hand or were able to do new construction with the skill and craftsmanship we rarely find today.

The furnishings and decorative accessories give the impression of belonging to the owner and are the things he likes rather than pieces chosen by an interior designer. There are items of personal memorabilia and pieces he has collected abroad or while shopping in local Connecticut antiques shops. The feeling is one of informal luxury that is successful because it does not call attention to the vast underlying effort and expense that went into capturing it.

The barn belonging to the photographer is perhaps the most radical renovation of the three we have seen. For its size it takes greatest advantage of the open space old barns afford. It is meant to be simple to maintain, uncluttered, yet somewhat formal. The owner has allocated a relatively small amount of space to his personal living needs. He seems to prefer to make the space available for entertaining many guests perhaps for an evening but few, if any, for a weekend. In spite of the huge undraped glass wall on the second floor and the room to accommodate many people at one time, the owner's emphasis is on privacy. By a combination of a secluded location, orientation of windows to the woods, and the lack of sleeping quarters for guests, it would appear that this desire has been fulfilled.

In common among owners of these three barns is a satisfaction, sense of accomplishment, and pride in their homes that I have not found in other homeowners. They may remember each nail as it was being driven and each decision as it had to be made whether to save or discard a particular beam or board. Or even if most of the work was given over to a contractor or an architect along with a blank check, they all share a similar dedication. Saving an old barn from oblivion, restoring it to usefulness, and creating a distinctive home seems to have its own unique reward.

Inexpensive remodeling job converted this barn and shed into an unpretentious vacation home.

Two barns converted into home and artists' studios. Older barn at left is husband's sculptoring studio and workshop. Family lives in more modern barn at right, which also houses wife's ceramics and batik workroom.

Master bedroom, which also serves as studio in which husband pursues his painting and graphic design.

Large industrial-type windows were installed in north wall of master bedroom to admit more light.

Architectural details from an older barn were incorporated into remodeled living quarters. This beam provides a decorative accent between kitchen and dining area.

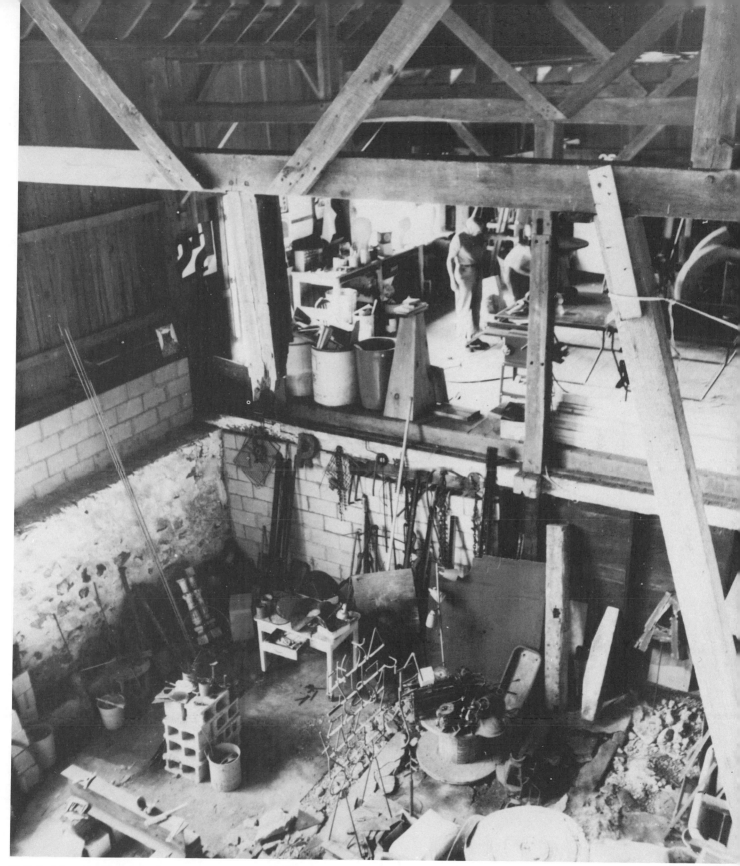

Full height of old barn was used for work on large-scale wood and metal sculpture. In the rear is woodworking shop. Saving this barn required raising the building and installing new sections of cinder-block foundation.

Two views of wife's ceramics and textile studio located in basement of newer barn.

The front of this barn in Roxbury, Connecticut, which faces the road, does not indicate the radical remodeling job that turned 150-year-old barn into a luxurious weekend home.

Seen from the rear, one gets a better idea of the size and scope of this renovation. Tall structure at the left is an unusual square silo, which houses owner's bedroom on glass-walled top floor.

Sixteen-foot-high Palladian window was bought for fifteen dollars and installed
by local craftsmen in a single day.

Living-room area looking toward rear sun deck. Floors were made from original chestnut boards found on the property.

At the front of the thirty-by-fifty-foot room is the kitchen and dining area. Stairs at right were built to reach additional sleeping quarters in part of former loft.

Access to master bath and bedroom in silo is through this doorway concealed in a section of book-lined wall.

Spiral staircase from bath up to master bedroom is new construction. It was built of old material by traditional methods without a single nail or screw: All joints were fastened with wooden pegs.

Barn was insulated and the interior finished by spraying all surfaces between the beams with a polyurethane foam. After the foam had hardened, it was painted white, leaving a stuccolike appearance that suggests the texture of the boards underneath.

Exterior of barn showing where insulating foam has come through openings where boards have decayed.

145

Entrance to remodeled barn in New Milford, Connecticut. Second story has floor-to-ceiling glass wall.

Rear of barn overlooks fern-covered riverbank. Chimney at right is new and serves fireplaces on first and second floors.

Two views of living quarters on first floor. Austerity of plain white walls and exposed beams is softened by graceful lines of French furniture.

149

Part of old barn door was hung on original rollers to close off kitchen.

Most striking part of house is fully opened second floor with its huge window-wall. Simply furnished sleeping area is at left.

Classically styled door frame and antique hinges were salvaged from eighteenth-century house under demolition.

Abandoned farms are surrounded with a variety of fences that need mending.
Barbed wire was nineteenth-century method of keeping cows in and people out.

154

Looking out through the openings of a ruined barn evokes the peaceful feeling of a cathedral.

Index